Looking at Countries

THE
CARIBBEAN

Jillian Powell

W
FRANKLIN WATTS
LONDON · SYDNEY

First published in 2006 by
Franklin Watts
338 Euston Road
London NW1 3BH

Franklin Watts Australia
Hachette Children's Books
Level 17/207 Kent Street
Sydney NSW 2000

ISBN-10: 0 7496 6476 2
ISBN-13: 978 0 7496 6476 3
Dewey classification: 917.29

Series editor: Sarah Peutrill
Art director: Jonathan Hair
Design: Rita Storey
Cover design: Peter Scoulding
Picture research: Diana Morris

Picture credits: Tony Arruza/Corbis: 25b. Tom Bean/Corbis: 8.
Yann Arthus-Bertrand/Corbis: 4. Jonathan Blair/Corbis: 7. Richard
Bickel/Corbis: 17. Pablo Corral V/Corbis: 25t. Howard Davies/Corbis:
16. Eye Ubiquitous/Hutchison: 18, 23. Kevin Fletcher/Corbis: 13. Owen
Franken/Corbis: 15. Stephen Frink/Corbis: 20. Philippe
Giraud/Sygma/Corbis: 19t. R. Hackenburg/zefa/Corbis: 26. Glen
Hinkson/Reuters/Corbis: 9b. Jeremy Horner/Panos Pictures: 27. Dave
G. Houser/Post-Houserstock/Corbis: 19b. Jonathan Kaplan/Still
Pictures: 10. Bob Krist/Corbis: 11, 14. Buddy Mays/Corbis: 22. Gideon
Mendel/Corbis: 12. Helene Rogers/Alamy: 21c. Galen Rowell/Corbis:
6. Superbild/A1 Pix: front cover, 1, 9t, 21t, 24.

A CIP catalogue record for this book is available from the British
Library.

Printed in China

Contents

Where is the Caribbean?

The Caribbean lies in the tropics, between the Atlantic Ocean and the Caribbean Sea.

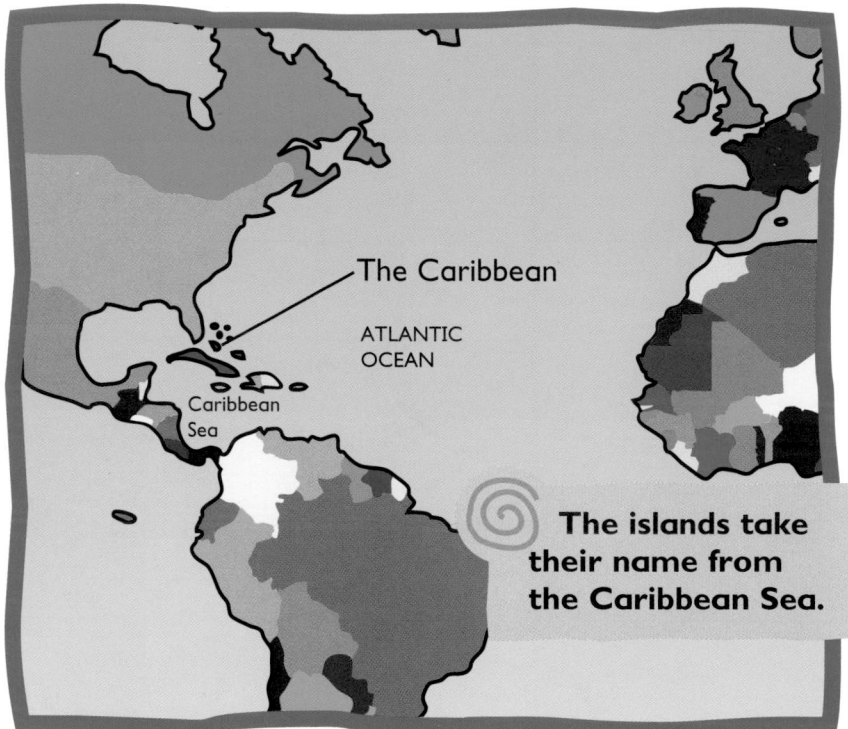

The Caribbean

ATLANTIC OCEAN

Caribbean Sea

The islands take their name from the Caribbean Sea.

The region includes over 7,000 islands, as well as the mainland countries of Belize, Guyana and Suriname.

The islands range in size from Cuba, the largest of the group called the Greater Antilles, to the smaller islands of the Bahamas, and the Lesser Antilles.

A view from the air showing St Vincent and the Grenadines.

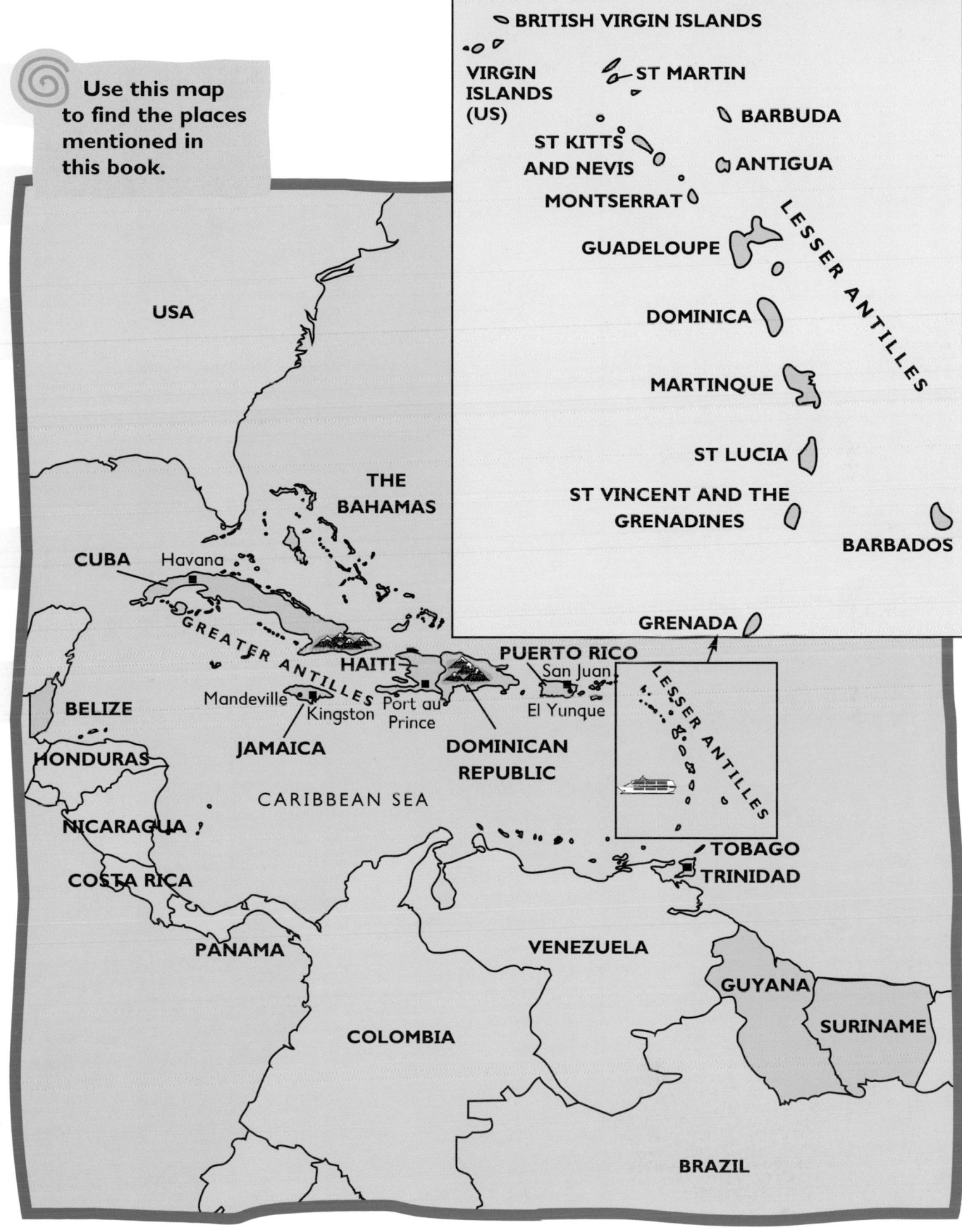

Use this map to find the places mentioned in this book.

BRITISH VIRGIN ISLANDS

VIRGIN ISLANDS (US)

ST MARTIN

BARBUDA

ST KITTS AND NEVIS

ANTIGUA

MONTSERRAT

GUADELOUPE

LESSER ANTILLES

DOMINICA

MARTINQUE

ST LUCIA

ST VINCENT AND THE GRENADINES

BARBADOS

GRENADA

USA

THE BAHAMAS

CUBA

Havana

GREATER ANTILLES

HAITI

Mandeville

Kingston

Port au Prince

PUERTO RICO

San Juan

El Yunque

LESSER ANTILLES

BELIZE

JAMAICA

DOMINICAN REPUBLIC

HONDURAS

CARIBBEAN SEA

NICARAGUA

TOBAGO

TRINIDAD

COSTA RICA

PANAMA

VENEZUELA

GUYANA

SURINAME

COLOMBIA

BRAZIL

The landscape

The Caribbean region is famous for the beauty of its landscapes, from high mountains to sandy beaches.

Many of the larger islands have steep mountains with lush tropical forests and waterfalls.

Mountain scenery in St Lucia.

Barbados is a flat island, with gentle hills inland.

Other islands, like Barbados and Antigua, have low-lying flat land. Some islands have salt marshes or swampy areas where mangrove trees grow.

The islands are surrounded by warm tropical seas and many have bays with coral reefs and white sandy beaches that are popular with tourists.

Did you know?

The beaches of Harbour Islands in the Bahamas have pink sand.

Weather and seasons

The Caribbean has a tropical marine climate. This means it is warm all year, with cooling winds blowing from the Atlantic Ocean and plenty of hot sunshine and rain.

During the wet season, from June to November, there can be heavy rain and flooding.

Tropical rainforest in El Yunque, the National Caribbean Forest in Puerto Rico.

The warm climate and beautiful beaches attract tourists to the Dominican Republic and other Caribbean islands.

In the dry season, from December to May, it is mostly very warm with showery rain.

Between June and November, there can be hurricane force storms, with winds of up to 300 kilometres per hour. These can cut power lines and destroy buildings and crops.

Did you know?

Each year hurricanes are given names that follow the order of the alphabet.

Hurricanes destroy whole cities and towns, as has happened here in Grenada.

Caribbean people

The people of the Caribbean are a mix of many races and cultures, from Europe, Africa and Asia. There are only a few whose ancestors were Arawaks or Caribs, the Amerindian peoples who were the first settlers in the Caribbean.

This man working as a logger in Guyana has Amerindian ancestors.

Many different languages are spoken on the islands including Spanish, English, Dutch and French. Some people speak local languages that are a mix of European or African languages, known as Patois or Creole.

Christians leaving a church service in the British Virgin Islands.

Many people are Christians. Others are Muslims, Hindus or Rastafarians. Some islanders practise African religions, and worship their own gods or ancestors.

Did you know?

Jamaica has more churches per square kilometre than any other country in the world.

Caribbean children

Most children in the Caribbean start primary school when they are five years old. They go on to secondary school at 11 and stay on to study until they are 15 years old. They may then study longer, train for a job, or start work.

These children from Haiti go to a school on a plantation in the Dominican Republic because their parents have found work there.

These boys are having a game of baseball in a back street in Trinidad.

Children from poor families have few clothes and toys. They make up their own games, sometimes using makeshift bats and balls.

The poorest children are the street children of Haiti. There are 3,000 in the city of Port au Prince. Some are orphans and have no homes, schooling or healthcare. Charities are working to help them.

Country

In the country, many people have small plots of land for growing root vegetables or keeping animals such as goats. Sometimes the women take produce to sell at market to earn some money.

Fruit and vegetables may also be sold from roadside stalls, and fish is often sold on the beach, fresh from the fishing boats.

Women in the Bahamas carrying market goods on their heads.

This sugar cane is being harvested in Martinique to make Caribbean rum.

Some people in the country find work on sugar cane, banana or coffee plantations. Some jobs are still done by hand pickers, although farm machinery is now used on many plantations.

Did you know?

The fruits and vegetables grown on Caribbean plantations are sold all over the world.

City

About three quarters of Caribbean people live in towns and cities.

The business district in Jamaica's capital city, Kingston.

The busiest places are the capital cities, like Kingston in Jamaica and Havana in Cuba. The capital cities have grown quickly. Many have high-rise buildings that contain banks, offices, shops and museums.

People crowd onto public transport, like this painted bus in Port au Prince, Haiti.

Did you know?

Havana has 'camel buses' (shaped like a camel's hump) that carry hundreds of people on board.

City streets are crowded with buses, trucks, taxis and bicycle taxis. These are often brightly coloured, like the painted tap-tap buses in Haiti, and the open-air yellow coco-taxis in Havana.

Caribbean homes

There are many different styles of home in the Caribbean.

In cities, many people live in blocks of flats in the suburbs. The richest people live in detached houses that have gardens, and modern facilities like air conditioning and satellite television.

School children on their way home to a block of flats in Havana, Cuba.

The poorest people in cities live in crowded shanty-towns on the outskirts. These have poor houses made from scrap tin and board. They have no electricity or running water.

A typical Caribbean board house, painted in bright colours.

These wooden houses in Barbados were built so they could be taken down and moved when families had to move to find work.

In country areas, most houses are bungalows, made from wooden boards with tin or palm-thatch roofs. They have verandas for sitting outside and shutters at the windows to keep them cool.

Did you know?

Mandeville in Jamaica has English-style cottages built around a village green.

Food

Caribbean food mixes many styles of cooking from Europe, Africa and Asia as well as the Arawaks and Caribs. 'Jerk pork', which is spiced pork cooked on a barbecue grill, is an Arawak dish from Jamaica. Spices are important in Caribbean cooking, and many dishes combine tropical fruits with meat or salted fish.

Street stalls like this one in Puerto Rico cook fast foods on the spot.

An open-air banana market in St Martin.

A supermarket in St Lucia offers a wide choice of fruit and vegetables.

People shop at outdoor markets and supermarkets for root vegetables, such as cassava, yams and potatoes, and fruits including mangoes and bananas. Rice and peas cooked in coconut milk, and soups or stews made with salted fish and root vegetables are popular dishes.

Did you know?

Grenada is called the 'isle of spices' – nutmeg even appears on the country's flag.

At work

In Caribbean cities, people find jobs in offices, shops, schools and banks or in factories processing food or making textiles. The larger seaports have industries for refining oil or cement. Some of these industries are growing fast.

An oil refinery and desalination plant in St Martin.

Tourism provides many jobs, on cruise ships and in hotels, restaurants and bars on the islands.

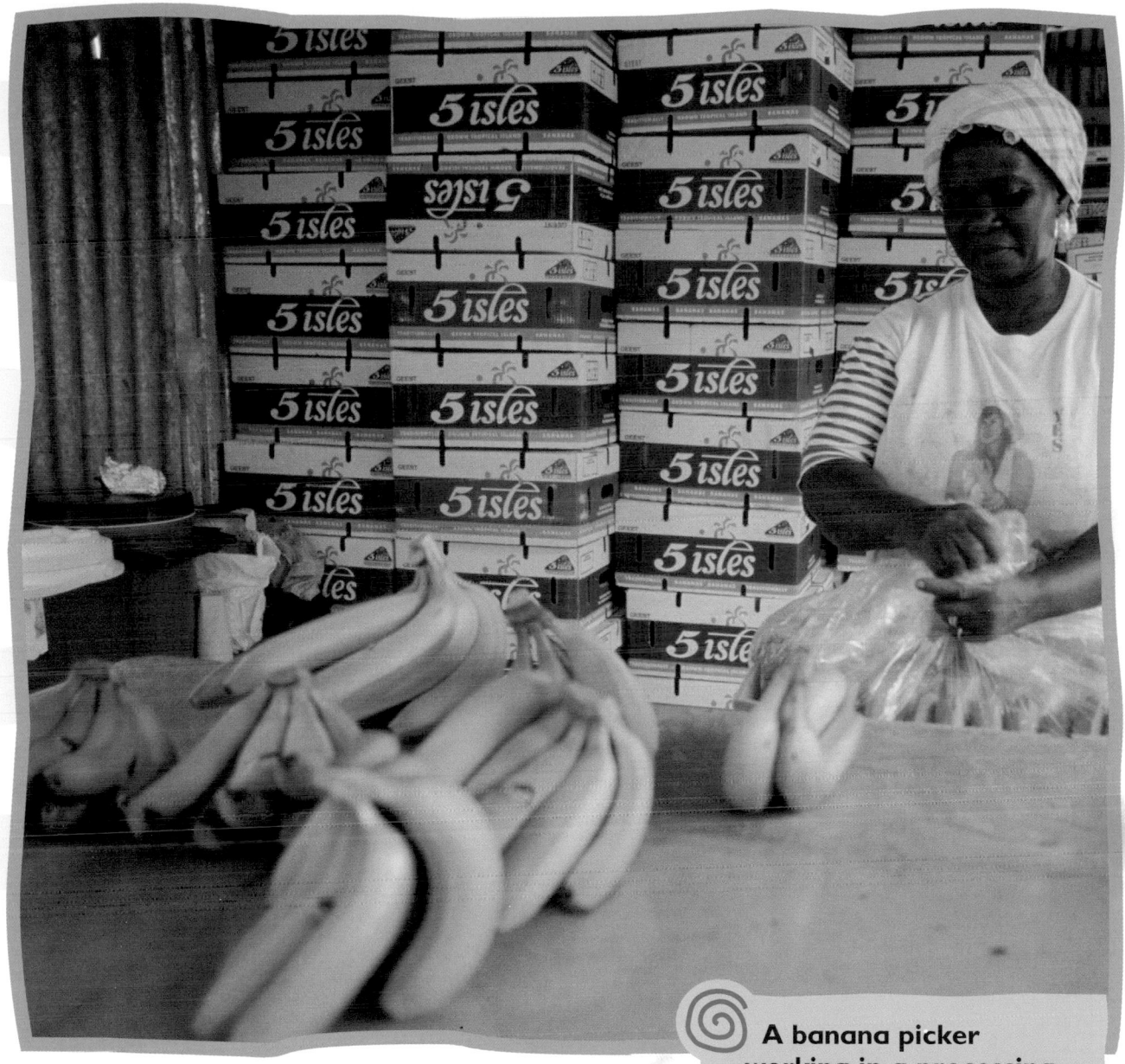

A banana picker working in a processing plant in St Lucia.

In country areas, people earn money by farming or fishing. On the coasts, they harvest foods like sea urchins and sea moss. Some work for big foreign companies, logging timber or working on sugar or banana plantations.

Did you know?

The Caribbean is the world's most popular region for cruise holidays.

Having fun

Caribbean people love festivals, music and dancing. Carnivals and festivals are a time for dressing up in colourful costumes and parading with floats through city streets.

Did you know?

In Antigua, people race crabs every week for fun!

These children are enjoying carnival time in Antigua.

Players in a steel band take part in a competition in Trinidad.

Steel bands, calypso and reggae are all Caribbean styles of music. In countries like Puerto Rico and Cuba, people dance in clubs, at bars and even on the street.

Sport is an important part of Caribbean life. The warm climate means that children love playing outdoor games like street tennis or beach cricket. Cricket, basketball, football and athletics are also popular spectator sports.

A game of beach cricket in Barbados.

Caribbean facts

- The Caribbean includes 32 different countries. Fifteen are member states of the Caribbean Community (CARICOM). The region also includes the Spanish-speaking states of Cuba and the Dominican Republic, and overseas departments of Britain, France, the Netherlands and the United States of America.

- The currencies used include the East Caribbean dollar, the United States dollar, and the euro.

Each country in the Caribbean has its own flag. This is the flag of Cuba.

Havana, Cuba, is the largest capital city in the **Caribbean** with a population of over two million.

• English, French, Spanish and Dutch are spoken on different islands, as well as Patois and Papiamento, which are a mix of African and European languages.

Did you know?

The Caribbean Sea was named after the Caribs, some of the first settlers on the islands.

Glossary

Amerindians original peoples of America.

Ancestors family members who lived in the past.

Calypso Caribbean song that tells a story.

Coral reef an undersea mound or ridge of coral.

Creole a mixture of different languages.

Cruise a holiday on a big passenger ship.

Culture ways and beliefs of a people.

Democracies countries where people have a free right to vote for their government.

Desalination a process to remove salt from sea water.

Export the sale of goods to countries overseas.

Mangrove a tropical tree that grows by coasts.

Orphan a child whose parents have died.

Papiamento a language that mixes African and European languages.

Patois a language that comes from English, Spanish, Portuguese and African languages.

Plantation a farm where crops like coffee and bananas are grown for export.

Reggae a style of music from Jamaica.

Salt marshes low-lying wetlands by the sea.

Steel band a band who play music on steel pans.

Suburbs the area around a city centre where people mostly live rather than work.

Swampy land that is very wet.

Tropics part of the Earth that lies close to the Equator.

Veranda an open area, usually with a roof, along the front or side of a house.

Find out more

www.globaleye.org.uk/ primary_autumn04/ eyeon/intro.html
A lively children's guide to the Caribbean with photos, quizzes, maps and topics including people, the weather and tourism. It includes a data file.

www.bbc.co.uk/video nation/feature/caribbean
A BBC website with videos filmed by Caribbean people talking about their lives.

Note to parents and teachers: Every effort has been made by the Publishers to ensure that these websites are suitable for children, that they are of the highest educational value, and that they contain no inappropriate or offensive material. However, because of the nature of the Internet, it is impossible to guarantee that the contents of these sites will not be altered. We strongly advise that Internet access is supervised by a responsible adult.

Patois

Many languages are spoken in the Caribbean. In Jamaica, English is spoken but Jamaicans have their own language called Patois, which comes from English and other languages. Here are some words in Patois you could try yourself!

Patois	English
al-a-we	all of us
bwoy	boy
dem deh	those
easy nuh	take it easy
gal	girl
irie	okay
Mi a-go lef today	I am leaving today
nuff	plenty
nyam	eat
oddah	other
whappen	what's happening / what's going on

My map of the Caribbean

Trace this map, colour it in and use the map on page 5 to write the names of the main islands.

Index